The Parables of Jesus

Ellyn Sanna

Illustrated by
Ken Landgraf

BARBOUR
PUBLISHING, INC.
Uhrichsville, Ohio

ISBN 1-57748-724-9

Published by Barbour Publishing, Inc., P.O. Box 719,
Uhrichsville, Ohio 44683 http://www.barbourbooks.com

 Member of the
Evangelical Christian
Publishers Association

Printed in the United States of America.

The
Parables
of Jesus

TWELVE-YEAR-OLD ZADOK WATCHED SOLDIERS MARCH BY.

1

The Kingdom of Heaven Is Like a Seed. . .

"I hate the Romans!" Twelve-year-old Zadok watched the soldiers march by and scowled. "When will Jesus make them go away? When will He set up His kingdom?" He looked up at his father as they walked home from the harbor where they had left their fishing boat. *Soon,* he hoped his father would say. *Next week. Tomorrow. . . .*

But instead his father only sighed and shrugged his shoulders. "I don't know, son."

THE PARABLES OF JESUS

Simon, Zadok's father, was a Zealot, a member of the rebel group that hoped to drive the Romans out of Israel. The Zealots believed the Romans had no right to rule God's people. They hated the Roman taxes, and when the Romans took a census of all the people who lived in the land, the Zealots refused to be counted. Zadok had grown up hearing his father talk with the other Zealots, and over the years, he, too, had come to hate these foreigners who ruled their country.

The Zealots also worshiped God and read the Torah, and Zadok had once loved to hear his father read to him from the Scriptures. Lately, though, Zadok thought less and less about loving God, and more and more about hating the Romans. He and his father worked hard on their fishing boat—but too much of the money they earned for their catch went to pay the Roman taxes. *It's not fair,* Zadok thought to himself as he scuffed his feet along the dusty street. They should overthrow the Romans

SIMON, ZADOK'S FATHER, WAS A ZEALOT.

now, before the Romans took one more coin from their pockets. Zadok wouldn't be afraid to take up a sword and fight. . . .

His father walked thoughtfully beside him, his gaze on the green hills behind their village. A few months ago Simon had become a disciple of Jesus of Nazareth, the new rabbi who claimed to be the Messiah, the one who would free their land. Zadok was filled with excitement whenever he thought of Jesus.

As they reached their home, Zadok tugged at his father's robe. "When you were with Him yesterday, did Jesus mention His kingdom?" he asked.

His father washed his hands and then settled himself at the table. He waited until Zadok's mother Lydia brought the last dish of food from the oven, and then, when they were all ready, he asked the blessing for their meal. Breaking off a hunk of bread to dip in his stew, he turned to Zadok. "Yes, Jesus did speak of His kingdom yesterday. But first He told us a story."

"JESUS DID SPEAK OF HIS KINGDOM YESTERDAY."

Zadok gulped down a chunk of meat. "Tell me what He said."

"All right," Simon answered. "Here is how the Parable of the Sower went. . . .

"Once there was a farmer, who was getting ready for the spring planting, just like all the other farmers. He took a big bag of seeds and hung it around his neck, and then he went out into his fields. Now he would plant his seeds, so that when they grew and ripened, he would have plenty of crops to harvest. As he walked through his fields, he scooped out handfuls of seed and tossed them from side to side across the dirt.

"Unfortunately, not all of the seeds fell on soft earth. Instead, some landed on the farmer's footpath. The ground there was hard and packed, not loose and soft like the plowed soil, and the seeds just lay there, not doing anything. Eventually, some birds came and gobbled them up.

HE SCOOPED OUT HANDFULS OF SEED..

"Meanwhile, the farmer kept on tossing his seeds from side to side as he walked along. And some of the seeds fell on rock that was covered with only a few inches of soil. Over the next few days, these seeds germinated and little plants quickly sprung up. But of course they did not last long. Their roots had nowhere to grow, so when the sun grew hot, they could not draw up any moisture from the earth. In the end, they wilted and died.

"But the farmer still tossed his seeds from side to side. Some of it fell on ground that was choked with weeds and thorns. The seeds tried to grow there, but before long the stronger growth pushed out the young shoots.

"The farmer still kept on throwing his seeds onto the ground. And some of it fell on soft, fertile soil. These seeds germinated and sank their roots deep into the earth. They grew tall and strong—and before long they produced a crop so enormous that it was thirty, no, sixty, no, even one hundred times

SOME OF THE SEEDS FELL ON ROCK THAT WAS
COVERED WITH ONLY A FEW INCHES OF SOIL.

as great as the number of seeds the farmer had originally planted."

Zadok wrinkled his forehead. "That was a strange story," he said slowly. He was trying to remember the farmers he had seen in the spring planting their crops in the fields outside town. Something about Jesus' story didn't seem quite right. "Why would a farmer plant his seeds that way? Don't farmers usually plow out the stones and weeds first, before they plant? They don't just throw their seeds up in the air like that, do they?"

His father smiled and shook his head. "No, most farmers don't act like the farmer in Jesus' story. But any farmer I know would be delighted if even some of his seeds produced thirty times as much harvest, let alone one hundred times as much. I don't know of any farmer whose fields yield more than ten times as much crops as seeds." Simon took a last bite of bread, then wiped a few

"ANY FARMER WOULD BE DELIGHTED IF SOME OF HIS SEEDS
PRODUCED THIRTY TIMES AS MUCH HARVEST."

drops of stew from his beard.

Zadok reached for the bowl of figs at the center of the table. He was trying to puzzle out the story's meaning. What had Jesus been trying to say? "So this wasn't meant to be a true story then?"

His father shook his head. "No, not true in the sense that Jesus was talking about an actual farmer planting his fields. But it was true in another sense."

"What do you mean?" Zadok took a bite of the fig.

"Well," his father answered, "when Jesus finished His story, He said, 'If you are willing to hear, then listen and understand.' I think He told us a story to give us a picture of what He was trying to tell us, a picture that would stick in our heads better than a long sermon. We could take that picture with us, and maybe we will spend the rest of our lives looking at it, thinking it over, understanding more and more what it means."

Zadok's mother stood up and began clearing the

"SO THIS WASN'T MEANT TO BE A TRUE STORY?"

table. "And just what do you think Jesus' story meant?" she asked her husband.

He leaned back from the table. "I'll tell you how Jesus explained it to us."

"When the seed fell on the path," Simon began, recalling Jesus' words, "where the dirt was hard and packed, that is like when someone hears the Good News about God's kingdom, but they don't under-stand what they are hearing. God's Good News can't take root in their lives, and soon the Evil One comes and snatches the seed out of their hearts. The seed might as well never have fallen on their hearts for all the good it does. It didn't change them even one little bit.

"The soil that was thin and rocky is like people who are delighted to hear about God's kingdom—but their roots are too shallow for them to truly grow. They are happy enough at first, but as soon they begin to have any kind of troubles or sadness,

"I'LL TELL YOU HOW JESUS EXPLAINED IT."

then their new life begins to droop. Pretty soon that life dies altogether.

"The seeds that were choked out by weeds and thorns are like people who do hear and accept the Good News from God—but before you know it, they are so worried about their problems and so busy taking care of their lives, trying to get themselves the things they want, they forget all about God. Of course those seeds will never have any fruit, because they just can't get enough nourishment. All these people's energy goes toward making others think they are important or getting lots of things or having fun. Those things take up their whole lives. They just don't have anything left for God's kingdom.

"But the good soil, the soil that is soft and rich, is like those people who open their hearts to God's message. And when they do, they grow so much that their lives make an unbelievable amount of fruit, more fruit than makes sense by ordinary standards. That's because the seed that God grows in

"PEOPLE OPEN THEIR HEARTS TO GOD'S MESSAGE."

our lives is amazing, spectacular, miraculous."

That night as Zadok sat in front of the fire, he found himself thinking again about the story Jesus had told. He wanted to have room in his heart for the Good News that Jesus talked about—but he wasn't sure what that meant. If the Romans were gone, that would be good news. Did Jesus mean that setting up the Jewish kingdom should be more important than anything else? That made sense; that's what all the Zealots said, too.

Or did Jesus mean something different? Zadok wondered. He looked at his parents as they murmured the evening prayers, and he thought to himself that they must be like the good soil. They were always praying and talking about God.

But did he, Zadok, have good soil in his heart? Sometimes lately he felt so confused and angry. Was his heart so hard that he would never be changed at all by the things Jesus said? Or was he so shallow

DID JESUS MEAN SOMETHING DIFFERENT?
ZADOK WONDERED.

that these new seeds would have no room to send down deep roots? He found his thoughts wandering, and he sighed, realizing that his thoughts were quite weedy a lot of the time.

Zadok turned to look at his father, who had picked up some fishing nets to mend. "Why doesn't Jesus gather an army if the Kingdom of God is so important to Him?"

His father's fingers moved quickly, tying the cord in strong knots that would hold the weight of many fish. After a moment, he looked up at his son. "I'm not sure I know. But let me tell you another story Jesus told us."

"Jesus told a Parable of the Wheat and Weeds," Simon began. "It went like this:

"The Kingdom of Heaven is like a farmer who planted his field full of good, healthy wheat seeds. He went to bed tired out but happy, knowing he had done his job well and that the wheat was all safely

"LET ME TELL YOU ANOTHER STORY."

planted in the rich, moist earth.

"But this farmer had an enemy, and that enemy played a mean trick on him. While the farmer was sleeping, his enemy came creeping through the darkness, a bag full of weed seeds over his shoulder. Quietly, the enemy planted those weed seeds right in the same field with the good wheat seed the farmer had just planted. And then the enemy crept back home, without anyone ever knowing the mischief he had done.

"But as the farmer's wheat germinated and began to send up little green shoots, so did the enemy's weeds. Pretty soon anyone who walked by the field could plainly see that it was full of both wheat and weeds. So the farmer's servants decided they had better let the farmer know he had a problem.

" 'Sir,' they said, 'you know that field where you planted the wheat?'

"The farmer looked up and nodded.

" 'Well. . .' The servants bit their lips, wondering

THE FIELD WAS FULL OF BOTH WHEAT AND WEEDS.

how to tell the farmer their bad news. Finally, one of them blurted, 'The field is full of weeds!'

"The farmer frowned. When he planted the wheat, he was sure all the weeds had been pulled out of the field—so how could it be full of weeds now? Suddenly, he remembered his enemy who liked to play mean tricks. 'An enemy has done it!' he shouted.

"The servants looked surprised; they had assumed the weeds had gotten into the field in the usual, mysterious way that weeds always got into a field. They had never dreamed that an enemy might have sneaked in and planted weed seeds in with the wheat.

" 'So,' one of them asked, 'should we go pull out the weeds?' He sighed, thinking how much work it would be to weed the whole field. His knees hurt just thinking about it.

"But the farmer surprised them even more now. 'No,' he said, shaking his head. 'If you do that, you

"SHOULD WE GO PULL OUT THE WEEDS?"

might hurt the young wheat plants—maybe even pull up the wrong plants by mistake. No, you might as well let both the weeds and wheat grow together for now. When harvest time comes, then I will tell the harvesters to sort out the weeds from wheat. The wheat I will put in the barn, and the weeds I will throw away and burn.'"

Zadok leaned back on his hands, his eyes on the dancing flames in front of him. "That's a funny story, too," he said thoughtfully. "You'd think that the farmer would have done something to save his wheat from the weeds. But instead he doesn't do anything. He doesn't even try to get even with his enemy. He just waits until the harvest." He turned away from the fire's heat and faced his father. "What do you think this story means?"

His father set aside his nets. "Well, Zadok, this is what Jesus told us when we were alone with Him later."

"THE WEEDS I WILL THROW AWAY AND BURN."

"Jesus is the farmer who plants the good wheat seed," Simon recalled, "and His field is the world. The wheat seed stands for the people who belong to His kingdom, and the weeds are those people who close their hearts to Jesus and choose to put themselves first. In real life, the enemy is the Devil, for he is the one who wants us to turn away from God's love and put ourselves ahead of anything else. Our harvest will come at the end of this world, and the harvesters are the angels.

"When the world ends, Jesus will finally send His angels, and they will pull out anything that makes people turn from God—and everyone who has chosen evil will be burned. These people will be in terrible pain; they will be sobbing and grinding their teeth. But the good seed, the people who opened their hearts to God, will be saved for eternity, where they will shine as bright as the sun."

EVERYONE WHO HAS CHOSEN EVIL WILL BE BURNED.

Zadok frowned. "Why does Jesus talk so much about love? Doesn't He hate the Romans? Does He expect us to wait for the angels to free us?" He yawned, suddenly sleepy. "I don't understand why God doesn't just take all the evil out of the world, right now, instead of sitting back and waiting for the end of the world."

His father nodded. "Some things are hard to understand." He looked up at Zadok's mother as she got to her feet.

"Time for bed, Zadok," she said.

Zadok nodded, but he waited a moment longer to hear if his father had anything more to say that would help him understand.

Simon sighed. "I get discouraged sometimes when I hear all the rumors about the bad things happening in our world. We Jews have little hope against Rome if we are not united—but I am afraid the Jewish leaders will never accept Jesus. I wonder where all the anger and bitterness will end. I

"DOESN'T HE HATE THE ROMANS?"

fear something terrible will happen, something truly evil. . . ." He sighed again. "But Jesus told us something else today about His kingdom, something that encourages me."

His wife put her hand on his shoulder. "What did He say, Simon?"

Simon gazed into the fire, his eyes thoughtful. "He said that His kingdom is like a mustard seed. You know how tiny that is, barely more than a speck. And yet from that tiny seed grows a tall plant, a plant that is as tall as a tree, a plant where all the birds can come and roost when they're tired." Simon smiled. "I guess when all we can see is little specks of God's kingdom, scattered here and there through our lives, we just have to trust that a tall, strong plant will one day grow from those tiny seeds."

As Zadok settled himself on his sleeping mat, he was still frowning. He knew God's kingdom still existed, in spite of the Romans, but he didn't know how to look for those tiny seeds his

HE WAS STILL FROWNING.

father had mentioned.

Seeds! he thought grumpily to himself. *What does a kingdom have to do with seeds?*

WHAT DOES A KINGDOM HAVE TO DO WITH SEEDS?

THE THOUGHT MADE HIM UNEASY.

2

*The Kingdom of Heaven Is
Like a Powerful Man. . .*

Zadok's father was gone for several weeks, traveling with Jesus. While he was gone, Zadok thought about all Simon had said about the Kingdom of God. Zadok wondered if Jesus would think that he, Zadok, deserved to be a part of God's kingdom—or would He think Zadok was a weed that needed to be burned? The thought made him uneasy, and he was anxious for his father to come home. Maybe when he did, he would be able to explain a little more about the kingdom Jesus would build once the Romans were gone.

At last, one afternoon when he and his mother were just sitting down to their noon meal, they heard a commotion out in the courtyard. Zadok hurried to the door and saw their donkey tied in his old place—and there was his father coming toward him! Zadok and his mother rushed at Simon with their arms open.

When they had all sat down and eaten, Zadok leaned toward his father. "So did you find out any more about God's kingdom? Will Jesus be setting up His kingdom soon, do you think? Will He get rid of all the Romans? Has He begun to build an army at last?"

Simon shook his head. "No, somehow I can't see Jesus leading an army. I don't think He will be that sort of king, son. Not a warrior."

"Oh." Zadok was disappointed. He loved hearing

THEY RUSHED AT SIMON WITH THEIR ARMS OPEN.

the old stories of the warlike Maccabees and the even older stories of Joshua. "Then what sort of king will He be? How can He get rid of the Romans without an army?"

Simon stretched his long legs, then patted his full stomach, smiling across the table at his wife. "I'm still not certain what kind of king Jesus will be. I'm not even sure I understand what His kingdom is like. He talks more about forgiving our enemies than about conquering them."

Zadok frowned. How could God want them to forgive the Romans for taking their land? Didn't God want His people to rule their own country again? "Did He tell you any more about His kingdom?" he asked eagerly.

Simon nodded. "Yes. I'm just not sure I understand. He keeps talking about the Kingdom of Heaven."

"Did He tell you another story?"

HE LOVED THE STORIES OF JOSHUA.

THE PARABLES OF JESUS

"Yes. He uses a lot of stories to teach us." His father settled himself more comfortably, then pulled Zadok's mother down beside him. "Let me tell you," he said, as he related Jesus' Parable of the Unforgiving Debtor.

"The Kingdom of Heaven is like a king who had loaned money to his people. One day he decided he should bring his accounts up to date, so he made appointments to meet with all the people who owed him money.

"Well, the first person he met with owed him millions of dollars. But when the king asked him where the money was, the fellow just shrugged. 'I'm sorry, sir. I don't have it.' He hung his head then, looking worried. 'There's no way I'll ever be able to pay you back,' he whispered.

"The king slammed his fist down on the arm of his throne. 'That's it! You've had all this time to pay me, and you haven't even tried to get the money

THE KING ASKED HIM WHERE THE MONEY WAS.

back to me. I've had it with you!' He turned to one of his servants. 'Take this man and sell him to someone who wants a slave. Take his wife and his children and sell them, too. Sell everything he owns as well, his house and everything in it.' The king shook his head grimly. 'One way or another, I'm going to get my money back.'

"The man who owed the millions of dollars buried his face in his hands and began to cry. 'Oh, please, your highness.' He threw himself down on the floor in front of the king's throne. 'Please, please,' he begged. 'Be patient with me! I will pay you back, if you just give me a little more time.'

"The king looked down at the man's shaking shoulders, and his face softened. He was too sorry for the man to be angry anymore. 'All right,' he said. 'You may go.'

"The man raised his head and peeked at the king between his fingers. 'You mean—?'

"The king waved his hand at him. 'Yes, yes,

"YOU MAY GO."

you're free to go. I won't sell you or your wife or your children or your house.'

" 'Oh, thank you, thank you, your highness,' the man cried. He scrambled to his feet and rushed to kiss the king's hand. 'You won't regret this, I promise you. I'll get your money to you as soon as I can. I should be able to get it by—'

"But the king interrupted him before he could finish. 'Oh, forget the debt. I've erased the whole thing. As of this moment, you don't owe me a cent.'

"The man could hardly believe his ears. He left the palace humming and skipping.

"But as he was on his way home, he passed a friend of his who owed him a couple thousand dollars, and suddenly he stopped singing and he stopped skipping. His friend was part of the reason why he had gotten into trouble with the king in the first place. Why, if he hadn't loaned his friend that money, he would have been able to make his payments to the king, he thought.

"OH FORGET THE DEBT. I'VE ERASED THE WHOLE THING."

"The man was filled with frustration and resentment. He reached out and grabbed his friend by the throat. 'Just where do you think you're sneaking off to?' he growled. 'Did you think I wouldn't notice you?'

" 'N-n-no,' the other man stammered. 'I was just—'

" 'Don't try to give me any excuses,' the first man shouted. 'I'm sick of hearing you whine. I want my money and I want it now.'

"His friend turned pale. 'Please,' he whispered, 'give me a little more time. I don't have the money right now, but I'll get it for you, if you'll just be patient. My wife has been sick, you know, and my cow died, and. . .'

"The first man squeezed his friend's throat a little tighter. 'I told you, I don't want to hear your feeble excuses. I'm calling the police to arrest you and throw you in jail. And you'll stay there until you give me my money!'

"I WANT MY MONEY!"

"And that is exactly what the first man did: He had his friend thrown into debtors' prison. But when people heard what he had done, they were upset, and some of them went to the king and told him what had happened.

"The king could hardly believe his ears when he heard what the man had done. Right away, he sent for him. 'You evil person!' he cried when the man came into the room. 'After I erased your debt, why couldn't you erase your friend's? You owed me millions of dollars, a far greater debt than your friend owed you. But I forgave you. So why didn't you forgive your friend?'

"The king shook his head in disappointment. And then he threw the man into debtors' prison until he could pay every penny of those millions of dollars he owed."

Lydia laughed as Simon finished the story. "I like that story."

HE HAD HIS FRIEND THROWN INTO DEBTORS' PRISON.

Her husband turned to look at her. "Do you understand what Jesus meant?"

"Of course," she said, smiling. "It's perfectly clear. We all owe God more than we could ever pay Him—and yet He cancels our debts. He loves us and pities us. So when God has treated us with so much mercy, we ought to forgive each other for the much smaller debts we owe one another. Instead of keeping a list of all the wrongs done to us, figuring out exactly how people ought to be treating us to repay all that we've done for them, we should just erase all our lists. Rip them into pieces. How dare we not forgive each other when God has forgiven us?"

Zadok frowned at his mother. "But what has that got to do with God's kingdom?"

His mother stood up and began clearing the table. "Well, it certainly is a very different kingdom than any I've ever heard of. I suspect it's a kingdom that wouldn't fight many wars, at least not the sort with spears and swords." She glanced

ZADOK FROWNED AT HIS MOTHER.

at her son's disappointed face and laughed, but then she sobered. "Personally, that sounds good to me, Zadok. I'm not in any hurry to have either you or your father going off to fight Romans. I would hate to have you shed anyone's blood. And I would hate even more to have you be wounded— or killed."

She looked from her son's face to her husband's. "When we can't forgive," she said softly, "then *we* are in prison. We're imprisoned inside our own hearts. Just like the two of you. You hate the Romans so much that I wonder sometimes if either of you will ever be really free."

Zadok rolled his eyes. "Why would God want us to forgive the Romans, Mother? He must hate them as much as we do." He turned to his father. "Jesus must have meant that we should forgive each other, our own people. The Romans aren't a part of His kingdom. Right?"

His father scratched his beard. "I don't know,

"WHY WOULD GOD WANT US TO FORGIVE THE ROMANS?"

son," he said after a moment. "I don't know." He sighed. "Let me tell you another story Jesus told us while we were gone." He glanced at his wife and smiled. "We'll see if your mother can make sense of this one."

So Simon began telling Jesus' Parable of the Vineyard Workers.

"The Kingdom of Heaven is like a rich landowner who owned a huge vineyard. The grapes in his vineyard were ready to be picked, so he got up at daybreak and hired some people to harvest the grapes. He discussed with the workers how much he would pay them, and they soon settled on a fair price for a day's wages.

"Later in the morning, the landowner was walking through the marketplace when he noticed some people standing around doing nothing. 'Hey, you!' he called to them. 'Would you like a chance to earn some money?'

THE GRAPES IN HIS VINEYARD WERE READY TO BE PICKED.

"The people agreed that they would be happy to make some money.

" 'Good, good!' the landowner said, clapping his hands. 'Go on up to my vineyard and get picking. At the end of the day, I'll pay you whatever is fair.'

"So the people made their way to his vineyard and got to work.

"The landowner went on his way happily, but then he noticed gray clouds building up in the sky, and he worried that rain might rot his wonderful grape harvest. So at noon he went back to the marketplace and hired more workers to pick the grapes. The rain held off, but just in case, he hired even more workers again at three o'clock in the afternoon.

"At about five o'clock that evening, he happened to be in town again, and he noticed another group of people standing around doing nothing. 'Hey!' he called to them. 'Why haven't you been working today?'

HE NOTICED GRAY CLOUDS IN THE SKY.

"They looked at him in surprise. 'Because no one hired us,' one of them told him.

" 'Well, I'll hire you,' the landowner said. 'Go on up and get to work with the others in my vineyard.'

"When night fell, all the grapes were picked at last. The landowner told his foremen to call in the workers and give them their day's wages, beginning with the last workers first. To everyone's surprise, those hired at five o'clock got a full day's wages. The workers who had been hired earlier in the day nudged each other, and their faces lit up. 'If those guys got all that for just an hour's work,' they whispered, 'just think what we'll get!'

"But when their turn came, they found that their pay was the same as the first group's. 'That's not fair!' they all cried. The ones who had been working since daybreak were especially angry. 'You paid them just as much for one hour of work as you did us who worked all day in the scorching heat. It's not fair!'

"IT'S NOT FAIR!"

"The landowner just smiled at them. 'Friends,' he said, 'I haven't been unfair. Didn't we agree this morning on a fair price for a day's work? Well, here it is. So take it and be happy. If I want to pay the last workers as much as the first, why is that any of your business? You have what belongs to you, and I can do whatever I want with my money. Why are you angry with me for being kind to these people? How does that hurt you in any way?' "

Zadok's mother sat down beside Simon and reached for her mending. "Doesn't that sound just like Zadok and his cousins?" she laughed. " 'It's not fair,' they always say. When I'm handing out the raisins or the sweetbread, those boys are so worried about who gets what, they hardly enjoy what they have in their hand." She chuckled. "This Jesus of yours knows human nature, Simon."

Her husband nodded. "Yes, He does. But why do you suppose He keeps saying that the Kingdom is

"TAKE YOUR PAY AND BE HAPPY."

like a person? His stories never quite make sense."

His wife took a few stitches, her face thoughtful. "I don't know," she said at last. "I don't understand, either. But that last story sounds as though we may all be surprised to find out just who belongs to God's kingdom in the end. We may find we are sharing the kingdom with people we never suspected would be there."

"Not Romans," Zadok said flatly, his face stormy.

"Who knows?" his mother asked lightly. "You might be surprised."

"But that doesn't make any sense," he protested. "They're the ones who took our kingdom from us. We can't share our land with them. We have to drive them out. How else can our land belong to God again instead of the Roman emperor?"

His mother shrugged her shoulders. "I don't know. But I wonder sometimes if our own leaders belong to God's kingdom any more than the Romans do."

"WE CAN'T SHARE OUR LAND WITH THE ROMANS."

Simon nodded, his face sober. "I think Jesus would agree with you there. You should have heard Him the last time we were at the temple. He told a story the Jewish leaders didn't like too well, I can tell you."

Zadok's mother laid down her sewing. "Tell us," she said quietly.

"Jesus told the Parable of the Evil Farmers," Simon began.

"Once upon a time there was a rich landowner who decided he would grow grapes on his property. So he planted the grapevines, and then he built a wall around the vineyard, to keep out the animals and thieves. Next, he dug a pit for pressing the juice out of the grapes, and last of all he built a lookout tower so that guards could keep watch over his land.

"When all that was finished, he leased the vineyard to tenant farmers and moved to another country. But when the time came for the grape harvest to

HE BUILT A WALL AROUND THE VINEYARD.

be ready, he sent some of his servants back to collect his share of the crop.

"Meanwhile, though, the tenant farmers had been wishing they could keep the crop all for themselves. They were hoping the landowner would never come back at all, so they could take over the vineyard completely. Needless to say, they weren't very happy when they saw the landowner's servants come walking in. In fact, they were so angry, they grabbed the servants and attacked them. They beat one of them, they threw stones at another, and they even killed one of them.

"When the landowner did not hear anything from his servants, he became worried. This time he sent a larger group of servants to collect his share of the crop, but the evil tenant farmers treated these people the same way they had the first group. Finally, the landowner decided to send his own son, whom he loved very much. 'They at least ought to respect him,' he said to himself.

THEY GRABBED THE SERVANTS AND ATTACKED THEM.

"But when the farmers saw the son coming, they laughed out loud and nudged each other with their elbows. 'Here comes the landowner's heir,' they muttered to each other. 'If we kill him, there will be no one left to inherit the land—and we can keep the estate for ourselves! Come on!' And they grabbed the landowner's son and dragged him outside the vineyard. There they murdered him.

"When the owner of the vineyard returns to his land, what do you think he will do?"

"Well," said Zadok's mother quietly, her hands in her lap. "I hope the Jewish leaders didn't hear that story."

"Oh, they heard it," Simon said grimly. "And they weren't happy at all. I heard rumors that they wanted to arrest Jesus after that story—but they were afraid to, because He's so popular with the crowds."

Zadok scratched his nose. "Did Jesus just end

THEY GRABBED THE LANDOWNER'S SON.

the story with a question like that?"

His father nodded. "Yes, He did."

"But what does it mean?" Zadok asked. "What was Jesus talking about?"

Simon leaned back. "I think, son, that Jesus was saying that the Jews have refused to listen to God's prophets—so God sent His Son to us. But if the Jews refuse to acknowledge Him as well, then I fear for what will happen. Maybe the landowner will take the vineyard away from the farmers and let other people tend the grapes instead."

"Do you mean. . . ?" Zadok struggled to make sense out of his father's words. "Do you really think that God would give His kingdom to someone else besides the Jews?"

Simon shook his head. "I don't know, son," he said heavily. "I just don't know."

Zadok was silent for a moment, thinking. "But we have listened to the prophets," he burst out at last. "Just because the Pharisees and the priests are

"GOD SENT HIS SON TO US."

bad, that doesn't mean we all are."

"No," Simon agreed. He smiled at his son. "And I don't believe Jesus would shut any of His true followers out of His kingdom."

Zadok put his chin in his hands, thinking some more about Jesus' story. One little piece of the story puzzled him especially, and after a moment, he lifted his head and looked at his father. "Is Jesus really God's Son? Not just a prophet, the way we thought —I guess that would be like one of the servants the landowner sent. Do you think He is God's actual Son?" The thought was mind-boggling.

A curious smile lit his father's face. "I'm not sure, son. I still don't understand Jesus much better than you do. All I know is this: He's like no one I've ever known before." Simon put his hand on Zadok's shoulder. "I guess we'll just have to wait and see."

Zadok frowned. "Well, I still don't understand exactly what Jesus thinks we should be doing to get ready for His kingdom. You'd think that even if

SIMON PUT HIS HAND ON ZADOK'S SHOULDER.

He's as mad at the Jewish leaders as He is the Romans, He would still want us to figure out how to get rid of them. What good do all these stories do? We ought to be doing something. Does He want us just to wait around doing nothing?"

Simon shook his head. "No," he said slowly, "I don't think He wants us to do nothing. I get the feeling He expects us to get busy now."

Zadok shook his head in frustration. "But what are we supposed to be doing? I don't understand."

His mother gave a little laugh. "Seems to me Jesus has already made it pretty clear—He wants us to get busy forgiving our enemies."

Zadok made a face. "That's no way to set up a kingdom," he said stubbornly. "It doesn't make any sense."

"No," his father said. "It doesn't seem to. Sometimes Jesus talks as though God's kingdom is already right here, all around us, and all we have to do is step out and claim it. And other times He talks

"IT DOESN'T MAKE ANY SENSE."

as though we shouldn't be surprised if we have to wait a long time before we see the reign of God here on earth. And then other times He speaks as though both are true at the same time." Simon shook his head. "He talks in riddles. But one thing is clear— He expects us to be working for the Kingdom now. If you listen to one more of Jesus' stories, you'll see what I mean.

"Jesus told a Parable of Talents," Simon recalled, then began quoting His words.

"The Kingdom of Heaven is like a rich man who was going on a trip. Before he left, he called his servants together and gave them each money to invest for him while he was gone. He had thought carefully about how much to give each servant, and he decided to base the amount on each person's abilities. He was a generous man, and he wanted to loan them an enormous amount of his wealth, so in the end he gave one of his servants as much money

HE GAVE HIS SERVANTS EACH MONEY TO INVEST.

as the servant normally could have earned in one hundred years of work, five big bags of gold. Another servant received as much money as he could have earned in forty years of work, two big bags of gold. The last servant received twenty years' worth of gold, a big bag filled to the top.

"As soon as the rich man had gone on his trip, the servant with five bags of gold went out and got busy. He invested his gold, and before long he had doubled it. The servant with two bags of gold also went to work right away, and before long he, too, had doubled his money. But the servant who had only one bag of gold was afraid to use it. So he dug a hole in the ground, and he hid the rich man's money.

"After a long time, the rich man came back from his trip. He called in his servants to see how they had made out with the wealth he had loaned them. When the first two servants told him they had doubled the money he had given them, he was delighted. 'Well done!' he cried. 'You are good and faithful servants.

HE DUG A HOLE IN THE GROUND,
AND HID THE RICH MAN'S MONEY.

And since you have done so well with this small amount I loaned you, now I want to give you still more. You will be responsible for an even greater part of my wealth, because you did so well with this.' He clapped the two men on the shoulders, and he spoke to them not as though they were servants, but as though he suddenly looked at them as dear friends. 'And now,' he cried, 'let's throw a party to celebrate your hard work!'

"Then he turned to the last servant. 'How did you make out?' the rich man asked him.

"The servant shuffled his feet, wondering if maybe he should have been more daring like his fellow servants. 'Well,' he said, giving his master an uneasy smile, 'I know what a hard deal you drive, sir. And I knew you wouldn't have liked it if I lost what you gave me. So I dug a hole and buried the gold. I was scared, you see, sir. But here it is!'

"The rich man's face grew dark. 'You lazy man! My wealth can accomplish absolutely nothing if it's

"YOU LAZY MAN!"

hidden away in the ground.' He sighed in exasperation. 'Here, give your bag of gold to this person
who has ten bags of gold. Those who use well what
they are given end up with even more, for I have
abundant wealth to share. But those who are not
faithful to me with a little bit of wealth, will lose
even that.' He turned away from the servant in disgust. 'Throw him out!' he said over his shoulder to the
other servants. 'He doesn't belong in my home.'"

Zadok hit his fist against his knee in frustration.
"What does this story have to do with establish-
ing God's kingdom? I don't understand. What
wealth has God given us that we should be using
for Him?"

His mother put a gentle hand on his arm, calm-
ing him. "God has given us much wealth, son."

Zadok looked around their small house. "I don't
see any," he said bitterly. "The Romans get it all."

His mother shook her head. "I see wealth the

"HE DOESN'T BELONG IN MY HOME."

Romans cannot touch." She smiled. "I see a family who has much love to share, both with each other and with those outside. I see three healthy bodies that have great strength for serving God and those around us. I see three pairs of hands for reaching out to those who ask for help, three pairs of feet for carrying kindness to those in need, three mouths able to speak words of love and forgiveness to all those around us. I see three pairs of eyes that see the beauty of God's world—and three hearts that can open themselves to God's presence in our lives. That is great wealth indeed, my son."

Zadok shook his head, but he bit his tongue against the angry words that threatened to spill out of his mouth.

Simon leaned forward and looked into his wife's face. "Did you hear this story from someone else before I told it to you?" he asked her.

She shook her head. "No. Why do you ask?"

"Because," her husband replied slowly, "after

ZADOK BIT HIS TONGUE.

Jesus had told this story, He went on to say something very similar to what you just said."

Lydia's face lit with interest. "What did He say?"

"He said. . ." Simon squinted his eyes, trying to remember Jesus' exact words. "He said that when we do something very simple for another, something like giving food to someone who is hungry, or water to someone who is thirsty, then we are really doing it for the Ruler of God's kingdom. If we give clothing to a poor person, Jesus said, or take care of someone who is sick, or visit someone in prison, or welcome a stranger into our home, then we do it for the King. And if we refuse to do these things, then we are actually refusing to serve our King."

A look of delight crossed Lydia's face, but Zadok still scowled, trying to puzzle out the meaning of Jesus' words. "Does Jesus mean that God is the King?" he asked his father.

His father sat back, a thoughtful look on his

"WHEN WE DO SOMETHING FOR ANOTHER, WE ARE
REALLY DOING IT FOR THE RULER OF GOD'S KINGDOM."

face. "I think," he said, "that Jesus is the King."

Zadok felt a flicker of relief. Jesus was a flesh and blood man, and if He claimed to be the King, then sooner or later He would have to set up His kingdom—and that meant the Romans would have to be overthrown. He gave a grim smile.

But his mother shook her head at his expression. "Think, son, what it will mean if Jesus is the Son of God. I'm not sure we can even imagine the sort of kingdom He will rule."

"JESUS IS THE SON OF GOD."

ZADOK HELPED HIS FATHER ON HIS FISHING BOAT.

3

The Kingdom of Heaven Is Like a Wedding. . .

Zadok was busy the next few days, helping his father on his fishing boat. After being gone so many days with Jesus, Simon was eager to bring in a catch big enough to earn the gold he would need to keep his family fed. While they worked together, father and son spoke often about Jesus, but Zadok noticed that his father no longer seemed as frustrated with the Romans as he once had. He seemed less angry, gentler, more thoughtful, and his new attitude disturbed

Zadok. *Maybe,* he thought, *Father would be better off if he stopped following Jesus.*

But a little voice kept interrupting Zadok's thoughts, bothering him. *What if Jesus really was God's Son?* What would that mean?

He tried to tell himself that if Jesus was God's actual Son, then He would have that much more power over the Romans. Even the Roman legions would never be able to resist a King who came from God. And yet Zadok was uneasy. He had a scared feeling in his stomach that things were changing somehow—and yet none of the changes were the ones he had looked for and hoped for.

After a particularly successful day of fishing, Simon left Zadok to clean down the boat and mend the sails, while he went to listen to more of Jesus' teaching. The next day as they set out to sea once more, Simon was unusually quiet. At last, Zadok asked him, "Did you find out any more about the Kingdom?"

SIMON LEFT ZADOK TO CLEAN DOWN THE BOAT.

Simon's eyes lingered on the horizon for a long moment, and then he nodded. "Yes, Jesus told us more stories about His kingdom. I think it's clear now that He is not talking about a kingdom for Jews only."

Zadok's lips pressed tightly together, biting back his disappointment. But then a new thought occurred to him. *Does Jesus want all the nations ruled now by the Romans to rise up together? To form a united rebellion against Rome?* The thought sent a thrill of excitement through him.

"Tell me," he said. "Tell me what Jesus said."

"Well," Simon began, "Jesus told a Parable of a Wedding Feast. It went something like this.

"The Kingdom of Heaven is like a king who prepares a great feast to celebrate the wedding of his son. The king is overflowing with joy, and he longs to share his delight with the people of his kingdom. He eagerly awaits the wedding day.

THE KINGDOM OF HEAVEN IS LIKE A
KING WHO PREPARES A GREAT FEAST.

"When everything is ready, he sends his servants to tell everyone to come to the party. To his great disappointment, though, the servants come back alone.

" 'No one wants to come,' they tell him. 'Everyone refused your invitation.'

" 'There must have been some misunderstanding,' the king says. He calls to some other servants, thinking that these people will do a better job taking his wonderful message to his friends. 'Go on,' he tells these servants. 'Let everyone know that the party is ready to begin. Tell them about the food I have prepared. Tell them what a good time we're going to have. Tell them to hurry!'

"But this group of servants has even worse luck than the first group had. At first people simply ignore them, going about their business as usual, working on their farms and tending their stores. When the servants insist the people listen to the king's invitation, they are full of excuses.

THEY ARE FULL OF EXCUSES.

'I have to go look at a field I just bought,' one of them says. 'I just got married myself,' another says, 'and my wife wants me at home.' 'I have to go look at some oxen,' yet another tells the king's servants. These are all such lame excuses that the king's messengers keep on asking them to come to the party, but then the people become angry with them. They attack the king's servants and beat them up, and they even kill some of them.

"When the king hears what has happened, he is furious. Now he sends out his army to destroy the murderers and burn their city. Then he turns to his servants again. 'I am ready to celebrate the wedding of my son. The food is on the table, and the party is set to begin. But the guests I invited aren't worthy of joining our joy. So this time, forget about the important people in my kingdom. This time go out to the street corners and the alleys, and ask everyone you see to come to

HE SENDS OUT HIS ARMY TO BURN THEIR CITY.

my party. Bring the poor people, the blind, the people who are sick. Bring people who can't walk, people who have no friends, people who are out of work and discouraged.'

"So the servants hurry off to do what the king asked. When they come back, one of them goes to the king and says, 'Your highness, we have done what you asked, but the tables still aren't full at the party. Would you like us to invite anyone else?'

"The king nods, and his eyes are bright with joy and love. 'Yes,' he says, 'go back again, but this time go out beyond the city into the country lanes. Invite everyone you see. And insist that I want them all, good and bad, poor and sick, everyone. I want them all to join us in our wedding celebration. I want my house to be full to the brim. But those people who refused my invitation will be left out; they won't even get a taste of the leftovers.' "

Zadok helped his father haul a net full of fishes

"INVITE EVERYONE YOU SEE."

onto the deck. But all the while he was sorting the gleaming, flopping fish, his mind was dwelling on Jesus' story.

At first he thought the story meant that his new theory was right: Jesus wanted to include in His kingdom the Gentile nations that were also oppressed by Rome's empire. That made sense to Zadok, at least in a way. After all, they would be stronger if they all worked together. His mind wandered off, wondering how they could organize themselves. And how would they make sure that the land of Israel belonged to its people? Would Israel rule the other surrounding countries, the way Rome now did?

Zadok liked that thought—but something told him this way of thinking didn't fit in with all Jesus had said. *Why,* Zadok wondered, *does Jesus keep talking about poor people and sick people, people who can't see or walk?* Zadok felt sorry for people like that—but really, what good were sick, weak

ZADOK SORTED THE FLOPPING FISH.

people when it came to setting up a kingdom? They couldn't fight. They couldn't really do much of anything, could they?

Zadok cast a sideways glance at his father, wondering what he was thinking. Before Simon became Jesus' disciple, he had shared everything with Zadok. Together father and son had plotted the overthrow of Rome, and Zadok had always loved to listen to his father talk with the other Zealots who were scheming against the Roman Empire. But now, sometimes Zadok wasn't sure what his father was thinking. Now that he was one of Jesus' disciples, Simon seldom met with his old Zealot friends. He was quieter than he used to be, and Zadok had the feeling he was lost in thought most of the time, pondering the stories he had heard from Jesus.

Zadok, suddenly filled with impatience, threw a tiny fish into the sea. "How much longer do we have to wait?" he burst out. "Jesus keeps talking about the

THEY HAD ONCE PLOTTED THE OVERTHROW OF ROME.

Kingdom—but when are we going to see it?"

His father looked down into his face. "I don't know, son. The things Jesus told us last night make me wonder. Maybe we will have to be patient for a long time. Maybe the important thing is to be ready, whenever the Kingdom finally does arrive."

Zadok's forehead wrinkled. "What do you mean?"

His father shrugged. "I'm not sure. Let me tell you another story that Jesus told us."

"Jesus said," Simon recalled, "that when the Kingdom of Heaven comes it will be like this:

"Once ten bridesmaids were waiting for the bridegroom to arrive at the wedding. The young women decided to take their lamps and go out to meet him. They would hold their oil lamps high like torches, and line the road the wedding procession took on its way from the groom's house to the bride's. 'Won't our lamps look beautiful,

"WON'T OUR LAMPS LOOK BEAUTIFUL?"

burning in the darkness?' they asked each other as they hurried out to wait for the bridegroom to lead the bridal parade.

"Before they went too far, though, five of the young women stopped to think. 'What if the bridegroom is late?' they asked themselves. 'Our oil will be all gone, and we'll have to stand there with unlit lamps. The wedding procession will have nothing to light its way, and our dark, empty lamps won't look beautiful at all.'

" 'Oh, come on,' the other five cried. 'Let's go. The bridegroom is sure to come soon. We don't want to bother with lugging along containers of oil with us. We might spill them on our pretty dresses.'

"But the first five bridesmaids shook their heads. 'You go on. We're going to bring extra oil with us, just in case. We'll catch up with you soon.' And they went back to get some containers of oil.

"They soon caught up with the other five bridesmaids, and together they waited for the bridegroom

"OH, COME ON, LET'S GO."

to lead the bridal party past them. But the hours went by, and still the bridegroom did not come. The bridesmaids began to yawn, and at last they curled up at the side of the road and went to sleep.

"At midnight a shout awakened them. 'The bridegroom is here! Come and meet him!'

"The ten bridesmaids sat up, rubbing their eyes. 'At last,' they grumbled. 'What kept him so long?'

"They reached for their lamps, so they could hold them high to light the road. But by now, of course, all the lamps had gone out. The five bridesmaids who had brought extra oil quickly poured it into their lamps, while the other five watched them sheepishly.

" 'Let us use some of your oil,' they said. 'Please?'

"But the first five bridesmaids shook their heads. 'We don't have enough for both our lamps and yours. If we give you oil, then our lamps will go out. No, you had better go to that shop on the corner and

"LET US USE SOME OF YOUR OIL."

buy yourselves more oil.'

"Sighing, the second group of bridesmaids hurried off to the seller's oil shop. But while they were gone, the bridal procession came by, and by the time the bridesmaids got back from the shop, everyone had gone on to the bride's house for the wedding feast.

"They hurried to the house and pounded on the door. 'Let us in, let us in!' they cried.

"The bridegroom came to the door, but he didn't open it. 'I don't know who you are,' he said. 'I can't open the door to strangers. Go away.'

"And the poor bridesmaids were left out in the dark and the cold, because they were not ready for the wedding."

Zadok scratched his head as his father finished talking. "I don't understand," he complained. "What is Jesus trying to say this time?"

Simon gazed out at the sea for a long moment.

THE BRIDESMAIDS WERE LEFT OUT IN THE COLD.

Then he sighed and turned toward his son. "I'm not sure, Zadok. But I think Jesus is calling us all to be ready for the Kingdom right now. And at the same time, He is cautioning us that we must be prepared to wait. We have to do all that we can to get ready— today, this instant. But we must be willing to wait for as long as it takes." Simon stroked his beard, looking thoughtful. "It's as though Jesus is saying two things at once, the way He so often does. 'Hurry up and get ready,' He tells us on the one hand, and then on the other, He says, 'Be patient and wait.' "

Zadok wiped fish scales off his hands. "I don't want to wait any longer. I want the Kingdom to come now."

"I know, son." Simon's eyes lingered on his son's flushed face. "Zadok," he said slowly, "would you like to come with me tonight when I go to Jesus?"

Zadok's heart gave a funny jump inside his

"I WANT THE KINGDOM TO COME NOW."

chest as he stared up into his father's face.

Simon smiled back at him. "The Kingdom is so important to you, Zadok. I think it's time you heard Jesus for yourself."

"I THINK IT'S TIME YOU HEARD JESUS FOR YOURSELF."

"MAKE SURE YOU WASH YOURSELF GOOD AND CLEAN."

4

The Kingdom of Heaven Belongs to
Poor People and Children. . .

"Make sure you wash yourself good and clean," Zadok's mother urged him as she handed him a bucket of clean water. "I don't want you sitting at Jesus' feet smelling like a dead fish."

Zadok gave his mother a nervous grin as he took the water. He was excited that at last he would see Jesus for himself—but at the same time, his stomach was filled with nervous butterflies. What would

Jesus think of him? Would Jesus answer his questions? He scrubbed his arms and face, and then ducked his whole head in the bucket of water. His hair dripping, he wiped his face with the towel his mother handed him, and then scowled. "I don't know what the big fuss is all about," he muttered. "He's used to fishermen."

"He's the Son of God," Lydia breathed, her voice full of awe.

Goose bumps stood up on Zadok's arms, but then he pulled on a clean robe and turned away. From all that his father had told him, Jesus was an amazing leader. But He couldn't really be the Son of God.

Simon stuck his head in the archway that led from the street into their courtyard. "Ready?" he asked.

Zadok nodded.

"Don't keep him out too late, now," Lydia called to Simon.

"READY?" HE ASKED.

Zadok rolled his eyes and hurried to catch up with Simon. "She still thinks I'm a child," he complained.

His father just laughed.

When they reached the house where Jesus was staying, they found a crowd had already gathered to hear Him speak. There were so many people that Jesus had come out into the street to talk to them; they would never have fit inside. Zadok was disappointed; he had hoped to be close enough to Jesus to ask Him questions. He and his father stood at the edge of the street, leaning against the wall, while Zadok tried to catch a glimpse of Jesus between all the heads.

Then Peter caught sight of Simon, and he grinned and motioned to him. "There's room for you and the boy up here," he called.

The crowd parted to make room for them, and Zadok found himself standing in front of a young

THE CROWD PARTED TO MAKE ROOM FOR THEM.

bearded man in a tan robe. "This is my son, Master," he heard his father say. Simon put his hands on Zadok's shoulders and pushed him forward. "Zadok, this is the Master. This is Jesus."

Zadok looked up into the man's face. "Hello," he said shyly.

The brown eyes searched his face, and Zadok squirmed inside, wondering what the man was seeing. Then Jesus smiled, and Zadok felt his heart leap. For a sudden, surprised moment, he felt as though he had just heard good news, something amazing and wonderful and better than he had ever hoped.

"I'm glad you are here, Zadok," Jesus said.

His voice was so gentle, that Zadok's eyes stung suddenly with tears. He blinked furiously. *How can a man with a voice that soft be of any use as a leader?* he asked himself.

Jesus smiled again, and one dark eyebrow raised. Zadok flushed, wondering if Jesus had somehow

"I'M GLAD YOU ARE HERE, ZADOK," JESUS SAID.

guessed his thoughts. He had so much he wanted to ask this man, but his father was nudging him to one side, and he settled cross-legged on the floor at Jesus' feet. He sucked in a deep breath, looking sideways at Jesus from the corner of his eyes.

He looked pretty ordinary, Zadok decided, noticing Jesus' worn sandals and plain robe. Jesus obviously didn't have much money, and that might be a problem. After all, money meant power, and they would need all the power they could get if they were to overthrow the powerful Romans. Still, money could be raised; the Zealots had often targeted the rich men who were secretly sympathetic to their cause.

Zadok laughed to himself then, as he remembered Jesus' claim to be the Son of God. *Why would the Son of God come to earth as a poor man?* It made no sense, and he wondered if his father could have misunderstood Jesus' claim to be the actual

WHY WOULD THE SON OF GOD COME TO EARTH AS A POOR MAN?

Son of God. For a person to claim to come from God like that, he would have to be either crazy—or evil, Zadok decided. He shivered, wondering if this man had somehow managed to totally mislead his father.

But then he darted a glance at Jesus' face. Jesus was laughing at something one of His disciples had said, and Zadok could see nothing in His expression that looked either crazy or bad. When Jesus glanced down and met Zadok's eyes, Zadok's face grew hot and he looked away quickly, his heart pounding. Something in this man's gaze made him feel different than he ever had before.

Jesus raised His hand then and the crowd grew silent as He began to speak. "I tell you, friends, don't be scared of those who threaten to hurt you. All they can do is kill your body—but they have no power to do anything worse to you after that."

His voice was firm and loud, and Zadok was surprised at its power. He smiled to himself. Maybe

JESUS BEGAN TO SPEAK.

this man would make a fearless leader after all. And these were good words to start off with, Zadok thought, words that would inspire the crowd to fight bravely against the Romans. But Zadok was startled when Jesus' voice suddenly became gentle.

"Five sparrows are sold in the marketplace for a couple of pennies," He said. "And yet each one of those sparrows is important to God. Think of all the flocks of sparrows in the world—and I tell you, God never forgets about even one of them. God cares about the small things, the things that seem unimportant. He goes so far as to count each and every hair on your head. So don't be afraid. You are worth much more to God than all the flocks of sparrows!"

The love and joy in Jesus' voice made Zadok suddenly wish he were a little child again. For some strange reason, he longed to turn his head against his father's shoulder and cry. "Foolish," he muttered to himself. "Don't be silly."

"EACH ONE OF THOSE SPARROWS IS IMPORTANT TO GOD."

Jesus was still talking, but Zadok missed what He was saying. Now a man in the crowd interrupted Him, shouting out, "Teacher, tell my brother he has to share with me the property our father left us."

Jesus turned to look at the man. "What gives Me the right to divide the property between you and your brother?" He asked. Then He turned back to the crowd. "Be careful about being greedy. Money is not important in My kingdom. Your true life has nothing to do with how many things you own."

How could money not be important? Zadok wondered. Could Jesus get soldiers and weapons without money? Money was one of the reasons why Zadok wanted to get rid of the Romans so badly; without the Roman taxes, his family would have enough money for a larger home, for fine clothes for them all, for gold dishes and soft rugs. . . . When the Romans were gone, a load of fish like he and his father had caught today would bring them enough profit that they could be nearly rich.

ZADOK WANTED TO GET RID OF THE ROMANS SO BADLY.

His father nudged him with his elbow, interrupting his thoughts. "Listen," Simon whispered. "He's telling one of His stories."

Zadok turned his attention back to Jesus.

"Once there was a wealthy man who owned a huge piece of rich, fertile land," Jesus said. "Every year the land bore so many good crops, that each year's harvest was bigger than the last. At last the man began to think to himself, *I have more crops than I can store. What am I going to do with such a large harvest?*

"The man lay awake at night, thinking about all he could do with the money he would get from his crops. This year's harvest had been so great he knew he would be wealthier than he had ever been before. 'What should I do with all my money?' he asked himself happily.

" 'I know,' he said to himself. 'I will tear down all my barns and build even bigger ones. Then I will

"A WEALTHY MAN OWNED A PIECE OF RICH, FERTILE LAND."

have plenty of room to store my grain. I will build a huge complex of buildings, so that I will have a place to keep all the things I am going to buy this year. And when everything is built, I will sit back and smile. "Lucky man!" I will tell myself. "You have everything you need. Take life easy! Eat, drink, and enjoy yourself!"

"The man laughed out loud as he thought these things. He rolled over on his back, his hands behind his head, and stared up at the dark ceiling, smiling to himself.

" 'Fool!'

"The soft voice made the man jump with terror. He sprang up in his bed, staring around the dark room. 'Who's there?'

"But there was no one there, no one but God.

" 'You fool,' the voice said sadly. 'This very night is the end of your life. Who will get all your money now? What good is it going to do you?' "

"WHO'S THERE?"

THE PARABLES OF JESUS

The crowd was very quiet as Jesus finished talking. He lowered His voice and added softly, "This is how it is with people who pile up riches for themselves and refuse to share with others. These people are rich in their own eyes—but they are poor in God's. And meanwhile, people who look poor to your eyes may truly be rich in God's kingdom."

The people began to murmur to each other, discussing the story they had just heard. Jesus turned to His disciples who were sitting closest to Him. "I'm telling you, you don't need to worry about things like food and clothes. Life is much more important than food, and your bodies are far more important than fine clothes. Look at the crows— God feeds them, doesn't He? And you are worth far more than birds! No matter how much you worry about something, your worrying doesn't do a bit of good. So why worry about anything? Your Father knows what you need."

Jesus looked down into Zadok's eyes. "God

THE PEOPLE BEGAN TO MURMUR TO EACH OTHER.

knows each and every one of you. He will give you what you need. You work for the Kingdom, and God will take care of you."

Zadok took in a deep breath, filled with relief. There—Jesus was talking about setting up His kingdom after all. Of course it made sense, he realized; if people were only worried about getting rich, they would never be able to work together to overthrow the Romans. Zadok thought of the Zealots who lived out in the hills, hard men who were willing to go without the comforts found in village life; these men were not tied down by the demands of a home and a family, and so they were more free to fight for their goal. Maybe Jesus wasn't so different from them. Zadok gave a Jesus a grin, longing to assure Him that he, Zadok, would never put riches ahead of the Kingdom.

Jesus returned his gaze gravely, and suddenly Zadok squirmed uncomfortably, no longer so certain he knew what Jesus' story meant.

ZADOK THOUGHT OF THE ZEALOTS.

"Will your son be with us again tomorrow?" Jesus asked Simon.

Simon glanced at Zadok. Zadok didn't know if he wanted to hear Jesus again; something about the man made him uncomfortable. But his father nodded his head. "Yes. We will both be here."

Zadok did not go fishing with his father the next day. Instead, after their morning meal, he helped his mother grind enough wheat to last them a week. He hated the job, and as he blew the coarse flour out of his face, he wished they had enough money to hire a servant to help his mother. If they didn't have to pay so many taxes, none of the them would have to work so hard. . . .

When his father came home at noon, they ate their lunch and then he and Zadok went once more to the house where Jesus was staying. They walked with Jesus and the other disciples up into the hills, a growing crowd trailing behind them. As they

THEY WALKED WITH JESUS.

walked, Jesus turned to Zadok.

"You have a sad face today, Zadok. What are you thinking?"

Zadok hesitated, embarrassed, and then he burst out, "I am tired of the way things never change. The Romans grow more and more powerful, and we grow weaker and poorer. Doesn't God care about His people? Why doesn't He do something?"

Jesus looked thoughtful. "Do you ask God to help you?"

Zadok kicked a pebble out of his path. "Why should I?" he grumbled under his breath. "God doesn't hear His people's prayers anymore. He only listens to those who have power."

He had heard his father say the same words more than once, but now his father frowned at him and shook his head. Zadok lifted his head defiantly. *Well, it's true,* he thought. He glanced up at Jesus' face, daring Him to contradict his thoughts. But Jesus only gave a small smile and

HE GLANCED UP AT JESUS' FACE.

began to tell another story.

"In a certain town," Jesus said, "—it doesn't really matter what town—there once was a judge who had no respect for anyone, not God and certainly not for other people. He was a hard, cold man, who totally lacked compassion.

"In the same town, there also lived a poor widowed woman who was having a legal problem. She had only a very little property to call her own, and someone was trying to take even that from her. She had no relatives to help her, and so she had no choice but to go to the judge and ask him for his help.

"But the judge was impatient with her little problem, and he barely listened to her complaints. The woman did not become discouraged, though. Day after day, she went back to the judge, and day after day she said, 'Please, Your Honor, help me. Take my side in this situation. I need your help.'

"The judge would wave his hand impatiently.

"PLEASE, YOUR HONOR, HELP ME."

'Go away. I don't have time for you. I don't even care about your problem. Go away.'

"But the next day, the woman would be back again. 'Please, Your Honor, I need your help. Take my side in this situation.'

"At last the judge threw up his hands in exasperation. 'All right, all right,' he said. 'I couldn't care less what God thinks, and I couldn't care less what anyone else thinks about me. But I am sick of hearing this woman's voice every day. I will take her side. Otherwise, she will just keep coming, and she'll wear me out.' "

Jesus laughed as He finished His story. "So, Zadok, if this selfish judge finally listened to the widow, don't you think God will listen to you if you keep on asking Him for help?"

Zadok stuffed his hands in his pockets, trying to understand what Jesus meant. He glanced from the humor on Jesus' face to the puzzlement

"I WILL TAKE HER SIDE."

on his father's. "Do you mean," he asked slowly, "that God will answer our prayers because He gets impatient hearing us ask for the same thing over and over?"

Jesus was still smiling, as though He had told a joke. "No," He said, "God is not like the selfish judge. God loves His people. But the point is this: If even that bad judge eventually answered the woman's pleas, don't you think a God who loves His people will take action for them?"

"I don't know," Zadok answered honestly.

"The question is, Zadok, do God's people really seek His help? Or do they try to do it all on their own?" Jesus met Zadok's eyes for a moment longer, and then He added gently, "Whose kingdom are you seeking, Zadok? God's? Or your own?"

Zadok opened his mouth—and to his surprise, he found he could not answer the question. His eyes dropped to his dusty toes, and he followed Jesus silently up the hillside.

"WHOSE KINGDOM ARE YOU SEEKING, ZADOK?"

THE PARABLES OF JESUS

When they reached the top of the hill, Jesus sat down and began to talk to the people. Zadok listened absently, his mind still on the story Jesus had told him. He barely noticed when a group of religious leaders pushed to the front of the crowd and began to ask Jesus questions, but he looked up when his father poked him.

"Listen to those men," Simon said under his breath. "They make me sick. They think they're so much better than the rest of us. You can tell from the way they stand there that they look down on us ordinary folk."

Zadok looked at the group of men in their rich robes. They held their heads high, and something about the tilt of their noses reminded Zadok of a group of caravan camels he had seen in the marketplace. He smothered a giggle, and turned to see how Jesus would treat these men. Would He be impressed by their power?

But Jesus seemed to barely hear what the men

ZADOK LOOKED AT THE GROUP OF MEN IN THEIR RICH ROBES.

were saying. Instead, He began to tell another story.

"Once there were two men who went up to the temple to pray. One of these men was a Pharisee, a very important religious leader who was powerful and well-respected. The other man collect taxes for the Romans, and everyone hated him.

"The Pharisee glanced at the tax collector, and his nostrils flared with distaste. Holding his robes close to him so they would not even brush against the other man, he moved past him, away from the other people who had also come to the temple. Everyone's eyes followed the Pharisee, and people murmured their respect, but he seemed to ignore them all. Instead, he turned his face upward and began to pray out loud.

" 'I thank You, God,' he said in a clear, carrying voice, 'that I am not greedy, like so many of the people here. Thank You that I'm not a liar, like some people I could mention, and thank You that I

HE BEGAN TO PRAY OUT LOUD.

have kept my promises to my wife. And most of all, God, I really, truly thank You that I am not like that tax collector standing over there. What a poor excuse for a man! I, on the other hand, as You well know, go without eating two days a week, so that I can spend more time in prayer. And besides all that, I always give You one-tenth of all my money.' The Pharisee's face was filled with pride as he finished his prayer.

"Meanwhile, the tax collector stood at the back of the room, too ashamed to even lift his face toward heaven. He was so sorry for all the bad things he had done that he beat his fist against his chest. 'God, have pity on me!' he whispered. 'I am such a sinner.' "

Zadok could see that the religious leaders at the front of the crowd were clearly displeased with Jesus' story. But Jesus only smiled at them blandly. "When the two men went home from the temple,"

"GOD, HAVE PITY ON ME!"

He said, "the tax collector was closer to God than the Pharisee. God was pleased with the tax collector's attitude—but He was not happy with the Pharisee's."

One of religious leaders reared his head back, and Zadok snickered, thinking again of a camel. "Do you mean to say," the man asked Jesus, "that God does not want us to pray and fast and tithe? That He doesn't care if we do all the things our religion asks us to do?"

"I'm saying," Jesus said quietly, "that if you think you are better than everyone else, you will eventually be put down. But if you humble yourself, you will find honor in God's kingdom."

People in the crowd began to shout out questions to Jesus, but He turned and wandered away through the people, stopping now and then to touch someone's shoulder, to smile and ask a question, to bend his head toward an old woman and listen to what she had to say. Zadok sat where he was, his

PEOPLE BEGAN TO SHOUT OUT QUESTIONS.

chin in his hands, wondering what sort of kingdom Jesus was planning to build.

He glanced up at his father, who was sitting quietly beside him. Simon hated tax collectors, he knew; his father had always called them selfish cowards who cared more for their own comfort than they did their own people, traitors who worked for the Romans and got rich from others' misfortunes. His father had no patience with the religious leaders either—but why would Jesus want a tax collector, even a sorry tax collector, in His kingdom?

Zadok was filled with a sudden, urgent need to understand. He got to his feet and followed Jesus through the crowd. He found Him sitting on the grass at the foot of the hill, surrounded by a group of children. Jesus was laughing out loud as the children crawled over Him, hanging on His shoulders and tugging at His hair.

Peter hurried past Zadok, scolding the children's mothers. "Call your children away! Don't

JESUS WAS SURROUNDED BY A GROUP OF CHILDREN.

you see the way they're bothering the Master?"

Jesus looked up at Peter and shook His head. "No, don't keep the children away from Me. The Kingdom of God belongs to people like these little ones. No one can be a part of My kingdom who does not have a child's heart."

Zadok stood as though he were frozen, staring at Jesus. What possible use would children be in setting up a kingdom? A child's heart could not plan battle strategies or fight to the death for freedom. In each one of the stories he had heard Jesus tell, Jesus pointed out a person who was weak or unimportant or humble—and then claimed that this person would be an important part of His kingdom. With a terrible cold sinking feeling, Zadok suddenly knew for certain that Jesus would never free them from the Romans.

Jesus settled a little girl in His lap, and then He looked over her head at Zadok. "Did you want to ask Me something, Zadok?"

"DID YOU WANT TO ASK ME SOMETHING, ZADOK?"

Zadok shook his head and turned away. He blinked tears from his eyes and pushed his way through the people. He wanted to find his father and go home. What was the point of listening to anything else Jesus had to say?

ZADOK TURNED AWAY.

SIMON SPENT MORE AND MORE TIME WITH JESUS.

5

The Kingdom of Heaven Is for the Lost. . .

During the next few weeks Simon spent more and more time with Jesus. He asked Zadok to come with him, and sometimes Lydia went, too, but Zadok had lost all interest in the teacher from Nazareth. Jesus was just one more religious leader, Zadok had decided. Jesus clearly had no interest in rescuing His people from Rome's power, and nothing He had to say was of any use to Zadok.

"But, son," Lydia said to him one evening as

they made their way home after listening to Jesus teach, "don't you see that the kingdom of which Jesus speaks is far greater than the one you imagine?" She looked at Zadok's stubborn face, and she sighed in frustration. "You're like a beggar who asked that someone give him one copper coin—and then is angry when instead he receives a whole shower of gold. Don't you see how silly you're being?"

Zadok scowled at his mother. "I'm not being silly," he muttered. "What good will this mysterious Kingdom of God do us if we are still oppressed by the Romans?"

Lydia shook her head. "What good would freedom from Rome do us if we are still slaves to our own sinful hearts?"

Zadok looked at his father, hoping Simon would say something to support Zadok's position. But his father was silent, his face thoughtful, and Zadok stomped ahead of his parents, impatient with them

"I'M NOT BEING SILLY," HE MUTTERED.

both. He longed for the days before Simon had become a disciple of Jesus of Nazareth, back when the world had seemed a simple, black-and-white place. Then he had known that the Romans were the enemy, the evil that he would give his life to fight. Now, against his will, Jesus was filling his head with new ideas, ideas that were too hard for him to grasp. He sighed with exasperation. And what good did it all do anyway? If they were all humble and simple, like children; if they spent all their time sharing their food with poor people and sick people; if they prayed all the time and said they were sorry for every bad thing they ever did—well, then the Romans would just get stronger and stronger, and the Jewish nation would be too busy being loving and humble to stop them. None of it made any sense to Zadok.

The next day, his parents brought him to hear Jesus again, and Zadok found he couldn't help but

HIS PARENTS TOOK HIM TO HEAR JESUS AGAIN.

sympathize with the religious leaders who were grumbling about Jesus. Jesus was surrounded by a crowd of people who looked like outcasts to Zadok, tax collectors and cripples, ragged women and blind children. Zadok shook his head at the ragtag group and wondered why he had ever thought that Jesus would be able to lead them to freedom. He found himself nodding in agreement when he overheard a Pharisee say, "Look at this man! He welcomes the worst kind of people. He even sits down and eats with them!"

Zadok had started to turn away when he heard his father's voice ask Jesus a question. "Who is the greatest in the Kingdom of Heaven?"

Simon had been so quiet lately, that Zadok was startled he would speak up like this. *Maybe he, too, is starting to question Jesus,* Zadok thought to himself hopefully. He pushed closer to Jesus to hear His answer.

"WHO IS THE GREATEST IN THE KINGDOM OF HEAVEN?"

THE PARABLES OF JESUS

Jesus reached out for one of the dirty children who were playing close to Him and lifted the child in His arms. "See this child? The greatest in the Kingdom of Heaven is the person who becomes like this little child. And whoever reaches out to a child like this, in reality reaches out to Me." He put the child down on the ground again and kissed the small head, then turned back to Simon. "Never look down on someone who is little and weak. These are the very people I came to bring into My kingdom." He glanced over at the group of religious leaders who had been listening scornfully. "I didn't come for the people who are satisfied with what they have already. I came to find the lost." Jesus turned and looked directly at Zadok, and a small smile flickered at the corners of His mouth. "Let me tell you some stories. Maybe then you will understand."

"Suppose you were a shepherd," Jesus said, "who spent your time out in the hills watching over your

"SEE THIS CHILD?"

sheep. You have a hundred sheep to care for, but one day one of them wanders away and gets lost in the rocks. What do you do? Do you say to yourself, 'Oh well, I have ninety-nine sheep left—what does one little lost sheep really matter?' No, you make sure those ninety-nine are safe in the pasture, and then you go out to look for the one sheep that is lost. You search up and down the mountainsides, late into the night—and when at last you find that one poor sheep, you shout out loud with joy.

"Gently, you lift the sheep up onto your shoulders and carry it back home. When morning comes, you call all your friends and neighbors together and tell them, 'Guess what? I found my lost sheep! I'm so excited to have it back. Let's have a party to celebrate.' "

Jesus looked from face to face in the crowd that surrounded Him. "In the same way," He said, speaking

"I FOUND MY LOST SHEEP!"

slowly and clearly, "I tell you this: Heaven is happier about that one person who is lost and turns to God than it is about the ninety-nine who have no need to repent."

Zadok let out a long sigh of impatience. Now Jesus was talking about sheep and Heaven, all in one breath, as though Heaven were an actual place that Jesus knew well. *He must be crazy after all,* Zadok thought with disgust.

Jesus met Zadok's gaze. "Zadok," He said softly, "I promise you that if you turn back to God, Heaven will celebrate. God longs to have you back. He doesn't want you to be lost anymore."

Zadok gulped, suddenly shaken. *But I haven't turned away from God,* he wanted to protest. *I'm not lost.* But then he remembered the long-ago days when he was small, when he had loved to pray with his parents before each meal and at the end of the day, when God had seemed real and wonderful to him—back before he had begun to hate the

"GOD LONGS TO HAVE YOU BACK."

Romans. He opened his mouth, not sure what he wanted to say, but before he could think of anything, Jesus began to tell another story.

"Once there was a woman who had ten silver coins," Jesus said. "She was a thrifty woman, who ran her household carefully, and she was saving her money for something wonderful. But one day, she discovered that somehow she had lost one of those silver coins.

"So what do you think she does? Does she say to herself, 'Oh well, it's only one coin. It's all right. After all, I have nine more.' No, each one of those coins was hard-earned, and each is precious to her. And so when she realizes that she has lost one, she lights a lamp and gets down on her knees and searches every nook and cranny of her house.

"And when, at last, she finds the lost coins, she sings with joy. She gets up and brushes off her robe, and then she runs out to tell all her friends. 'I'm so

"WHEN SHE FINDS THE LOST COINS, SHE SINGS WITH JOY."

happy!' she cries. 'Come over to my house and celebrate with me.'"

Jesus fell silent. Then He added softly, "I tell you, Zadok, the angels of God rejoice in the same way when a sinner comes back to God."

Somehow, Zadok could not make himself look into Jesus' face. He hung his head, thinking, *First it's sheep and Heaven, and now it's housewives and angels. He's crazy. He doesn't make any sense. None of this is important.* But somehow his heart told him that Jesus' words *were* important. He had a dizzy, uncomfortable feeling, as though everything he had believed for so long was crumbling around him. He raised his head and searched the crowd for his mother's face. When he found it, she was already looking at him, her eyes filled with such love that he blinked and looked away, embarrassed.

"I have one more story, Zadok," Jesus said,

"I HAVE ONE MORE STORY, ZADOK."

and then He raised His voice so that everyone could hear.

"There was once a man who had two sons. The older one was hard working and responsible, but the younger one was only interested in enjoying himself and having a good time.

"One day the younger son came to his father and said, 'Father, I don't want to wait until you die for my share of your property. Give it to me now.'

"So the father, who loved his sons very much, divided his property between the two young men.

"Only a few days later, the younger son took his share of the property and sold it. His father's heart broke as he watched his son pack his bags and leave home, but he did nothing to stop the young man.

"The younger son went down the road whistling, glad to leave behind the life he had lived in his father's house. He traveled to a distant country, and there he had a good time, spending his money

THE YOUNGER SON TRAVELED TO A DISTANT COUNTRY.

on anything and everything. Before long, he had spent every cent of the sizable fortune his father had given him.

"At about the same time, a terrible famine hit the country where he was staying. There was not enough food to go around, even for those who had money, and the younger son had nothing. Desperate, he got a job with a farmer, who sent him to take care of his pigs.

"The young man's stomach was growling, and he was dizzy with hunger, but no one offered him anything to eat; apparently, he was expected to earn his food first. He was so desperate for food that he started to cram the pig food in his mouth, but one of the other workers saw him. 'Hey, you!' the other worker shouted. 'Stop that. The farmer won't like it if he hears you've been eating the food meant to fatten his pigs.'

"At that moment, the young man came to his senses. *My father's workers all have as much food*

HE TOOK CARE OF PIGS.

as they want, he thought to himself, *and here I am starving to death. I might as well go back home.* As he shoveled out the pigsty, he planned the speech he would say to his father when he got home. 'Father,' he would say, 'I have sinned against God and against you. I'm no longer fit to be called your son, so please, treat me now like one of your hired workers.'

"He threw down his shovel and left the pig farm, suddenly so eager to be home that he could wait no longer.

"When he was still a long way down the road from his father's house, he saw someone running toward him. It was his father, running like a strong, young man, his robe blowing out behind him, his arms outstretched. 'Son,' he called. 'Son!' He reached the young man and threw his arms around him and kissed him.

"The young man immediately launched into his planned speech. 'Father, I have sinned against God

"SON," HE CALLED. "SON!"

and against you. I'm no longer fit to be called your son, so—'

"But before he could get any further, his father interrupted him by calling over his shoulder to his servants. 'Quick!' his father shouted. 'Go get some good clothes to put on my son. Get my gold ring out and put it on his finger. Put some shoes on his feet. And then go kill that calf we've been fattening up for a special occasion. We're going to have a party!' He turned back to his son with tears in his eyes, and his voice was tender now. 'For this son of mine was dead, but now he is alive. He was lost, but now I have found him again.'

"He gave his son another hug, and then the party began.

"But meanwhile the older son had been working hard for his father during all the time the younger son was away. Now, as he came in from working in the field, he could hear the music and dancing from inside the house. 'What's going on?'

THE PARTY BEGAN.

he called to one of the servants.

" 'Your brother has come back,' the servant answered. 'Your father is so happy to have him home safe and sound, he's thrown a big party. He even killed that prize calf of his he's been saving.'

"When the older son heard this, he was filled with anger and jealousy. He was so upset that he refused to even go inside the house.

"But his father came out to him. 'Please, son, come inside and celebrate with us. Your brother is home!'

"The older brother bit his lip to keep back his rage. When he had himself under control, he said between his teeth, 'Look, all these years I have worked for you without ever complaining. I work as hard as any of your hired workers, and I have never once disobeyed you. And what have you given me? Nothing. You've never suggested that I throw even a little party for my friends. But when my little brother runs off with his inheritance and then comes

"I HAVE NEVER ONCE DISOBEYED YOU."

back with nothing, what do you do? You kill your prize calf and throw an enormous party. You always did like him best. It's not fair.'

"His father couldn't help but laugh, even as he reached out and put his arm around his older son. 'Don't be silly, son,' he said. 'You have your inheritance, just as your brother did. You and I are always together, and being with you makes me happy every day. Everything I have is yours. But today we are celebrating because your brother who was lost is found at last. I thought he was dead, but instead he is home and safe. Be happy with us, son. You know how much I love you.' "

Zadok and his parents were quiet as they walked home that evening. As they reached their house, Lydia said softly, "What do you think the older brother did?"

"What do you mean?" Zadok asked her as he followed her inside.

"WHAT DO YOU THNK THE OLDER BROTHER DID?"

"When his father told him how much he loved him and asked him to celebrate with him." She began to get out the food for their supper. "Do you think the older brother joined the party? Or do you think he still refused to come inside?"

Simon lit the fire. "I hope he had enough sense to come inside with his father. Anger and hatred are poor companions, I've learned. They eat you up inside and leave you with nothing."

Lydia smiled up at her husband, then reached to press a kiss against his cheek. "You've changed, Simon," she said.

He looked back at her. "I suppose I have." He glanced at his son and added, "I thought I had to change the world by overthrowing the Roman government. But Jesus has taught me that the most important change has to happen inside my own heart."

Zadok looked back and forth between his parents. The quiet joy he saw in their faces filled

"DO YOU THINK THE OLDER BROTHER JOINED THE PARTY?"

him with rage. What good would all this love and gentleness do anyone? It wouldn't put food on their table or pay their taxes. It would leave the smug Romans in power, and the Jews would be as poor as ever.

He wanted to shout at them and make them see how wrong they were. But it wasn't their fault, he realized; it was Jesus of Nazareth who had confused them.

Zadok pressed his lips tight together. The next time he saw Jesus, Zadok was going to speak his mind.

HE WANTED TO MAKE THEM SEE HOW WRONG THEY WERE.

"WELL, ZADOK?"

6

The Kingdom of God Is Within You. . .

Zadok had his chance the next week when his parents again went to sit at Jesus' feet and listen to Him teach. As soon as they were settled, Jesus leaned forward and looked into Zadok's eyes, as if He knew Zadok had something he wanted to say. "Well, Zadok?"

Zadok felt his face turn red, but he raised his chin and said, "My father followed You at first because he thought You were the one we were waiting for, the Messiah, the one who would lead us to freedom. But he was wrong." His mother kicked him in the back with her sandal, but he ignored her and held his ground, his head high. "Just what sort of kingdom do You think all Your talk will lead to?"

Jesus looked into Zadok's face calmly. "An eternal kingdom, Zadok. A kingdom that lasts forever. A kingdom where you will never die."

His answer took Zadok by surprise. Zadok gulped and fell silent. He tried to think of a response, something that would get the conversation back on track, but before he could say anything a teacher of Jewish Law stepped forward and asked, "Teacher, what act must I perform to live forever?"

Jesus turned toward the man. "Well, what do the Scriptures say? How do you interpret them?"

The man answered immediately, "The Scriptures say to love the Lord your God with all your heart, with all your soul, with all your strength, and with all your mind." He obviously knew this answer

"TEACHER, WHAT ACT MUST I PERFORM TO LIVE FOREVER?"

by heart. "And," he added, "love your neighbor as yourself."

"That's right," Jesus replied. "Keep on doing this and you will live forever."

The teacher of the Law shifted his weight from foot to foot. "Well, then," he asked uncomfortably, "who is my neighbor?"

Jesus smiled. "That's a good question. Let Me tell you a story."

"There was once a man," Jesus said, "who was traveling the dangerous road between Jerusalem and Jericho. As happens to so many travelers along that road, he was attacked by robbers who beat him up, took everything he had, and then left him half-dead beside the road.

"A priest came along the road. He saw the injured man lying there all bloody, but he knew he would get himself dirty if he touched the man. 'Surely,' he said to himself, 'God doesn't want me

A PRIEST CAME ALONG THE ROAD.

to touch this man. He could be someone who isn't a Jew, or he could be dead. I would be breaking the law if I touched him. I have just come from serving God in the temple, and it would be bad for my spiritual condition if I lowered myself by getting mixed up with this terrible situation.'

"And so the priest crossed to the other side of the road and hurried on by.

"Next, one of the temple helpers came along the road. He stopped for a moment and looked at the wounded man, but the man looked so terrible lying there covered with blood that the temple helper could not bring himself to touch him. He, too, hurried across the road and went on his way, leaving the man alone and in agony.

"But before long a man from Samaria came down the road. Of course, the Jews hate Samaritans and think they are all violent and dangerous, but when this Samaritan saw the wounded man, his heart was filled with pity. He immediately went to

ONE OF THE TEMPLE HELPERS LOOKED AT THE WOUNDED MAN.

him and bent down to help him. He put medicine and bandages on his wounds, and then he lifted him onto his donkey. The Samaritan took the wounded man to an inn, and there he cared for him until the man was well enough for the Samaritan to leave him. Before the Samaritan left, he gave enough money to the innkeeper to provide for the man until he was totally recovered."

Jesus looked at the teacher of the Law. "Which of these three men would you say was a neighbor to the wounded man?"

The teacher looked down at the ground. "The one who showed real love," he said in a low voice.

"Exactly," Jesus agreed. "Now if you want live forever, you go and do the same."

The teacher stood still for a moment, looking as though he wanted to say something and yet could not quite bring himself to speak the words out loud. At last, with a sigh, he walked away.

"YOU GO AND DO THE SAME."

Jesus looked after him for a moment, and then He turned back to Zadok. "Do you want to live forever, Zadok?"

Zadok shrugged, though his heart was beating hard. "No one lives forever."

Jesus shook His head. "In My kingdom, Zadok, no one dies." He smiled. "You have had your eyes fixed on an earthly kingdom, one where the Jews would be free of Roman power. But all along, I have been talking about a heavenly kingdom, one that is far greater than anything you could ever imagine. Which kingdom do you choose, Zadok?"

For some reason, Zadok felt his eyes burn. He stared straight ahead. "When will this kingdom of Yours come then?" he asked, his voice hard and flat.

Jesus shook His head again. "No, Zadok, you're still thinking of another sort of kingdom. My kingdom is not made of something you can see and touch. You won't be able to say, 'Here it is!' or 'Look, it's over there!' The Kingdom of God here,

"DO YOU WANT TO LIVE FOREVER, ZADOK?"

Zadok." Jesus stretched out His hand and touched first Zadok's heart and then his forehead. "It is within you."

"I don't understand," Zadok whispered. He blinked away the tears that threatened to spill out of his eyes.

"It's not so complicated, really," Jesus said gently. "Think about the story I just told you. How can your heart lead you to the Kingdom of Heaven?"

Zadok looked into Jesus' dark eyes and he saw the love there. He felt his mother close beside him, and then his father's hand dropped on his shoulder. He knew he was surrounded by love. Was this the Kingdom that Jesus talked about?

But he had hated the Romans so long. How could he allow Jesus to take that hatred out of his heart? What would there be to take its place? All he had wanted was freedom for their nation. Who would he be if he allowed something else to be more important to him? He looked up doubtfully

"THINK ABOUT THE STORY I JUST TOLD YOU."

from his mother to his father, trying to see the answer in their faces.

"It's simple," his mother said. "Love is what leads you to the Kingdom of Heaven."

His father's hand squeezed his shoulder tight. "I'm sorry, son, that I confused you with my own anger against the Romans. I still want freedom for our nation. But your mother is right. Love is the most important thing—like the teacher of the Law just said. If you love God with all your heart and soul and mind you will give yourself to Him. And if you love your neighbor, then you treat everyone you meet with the same concern you would want them to show you. Doing that is more important than how much money we have or what kind of clothes we wear." Simon looked at Jesus. "If I understand right, love is the door that leads us into the Master's kingdom—and His kingdom will last forever. Not even death can end it."

Zadok turned from his parents to Jesus. He

"LOVE IS WHAT LEADS YOU TO THE KINGDOM OF HEAVEN."

thought of all of Jesus' stories, and suddenly they all began to make sense. Jesus nodded. "Come back to Me, Zadok. Give your heart away. Be a part of My kingdom. Will you?"

For a moment, Zadok was too scared to say anything. But then he looked into Jesus' eyes, and his fear disappeared. He took a deep breath. "Yes," he said, and he saw Jesus' face fill with joy.

HE LOOKED INTO JESUS' EYES.

AWESOME BOOKS FOR KIDS!

The Young Reader's Christian Library
Action, Adventure, and Fun Reading!

This series for young readers ages 8 to 12 is action-packed, fast-paced, and Christ-centered! With exciting illustrations on every other page following the text, kids won't be able to put these books down! Over 100 illustrations per book. All books are paperbound. The unique size (4 ⅛" x 5 ⅜") makes these books easy to take anywhere!

A Great Selection to Satisfy All Kids!

Abraham Lincoln

Billy Graham

Christopher
  Columbus

Clara Barton

Corrie ten Boom

Daniel

David

David Livingstone

Deborah

Elijah

Esther

Florence
  Nightingale

Harriet Tubman

Hudson Taylor

In His Steps

Jesus

Jim Elliot

Joseph

Little Women

Luis Palau

Lydia

Mary, Mother of
  Jesus

Miriam

Moses

Noah

Paul

Peter

The Pilgrim's
  Progress

Roger Williams

Ruth

Samuel

Samuel Morris

Sojourner Truth